To the Ends of the Earth

Mission Stories from Around the World

As Told by Marj Carpenter

Edited by Kent Chrisman

Presbyterian Publishing Corporation
Louisville, Kentucky

Book design by Pip Pullen

Cover illustration and design by Pip Pullen

First edition

Published by Presbyterian Publishing Corporation

This book is printed on acid-free paper
that meets the American National Standards Institute Z39.48 standard.

PRINTED IN THE UNITED STATES OF AMERICA

ISBN 1–57153–942–5

To the Ends of the Earth

Contents

Preface

The Church of Jesus Christ is alive and well in the world and the Presbyterian family is a very important part of that. The Presbyterians have opened more mission fields than any other church in history. We have taken very seriously the commission to go into all nations and take the gospel to all people, and we don't even known we've done it. Actually, of any church I know, the Presbyterians have done the best job of taking mission out into all the world, but the Presbyterians have also done the worst job of relating to their own denomination what they have done well. As I have gone around the church telling stories about missions, many people have asked me to put these stories down so they can share them with others. I rejoice that they want to do this.

What Do We Do in the World?

The very first place I went to see mission work was Brazil, and I ended up on a beach in Fortaleza. It should have been a beautiful beach, but it wasn't because people were living there in a packing-crate village under pieces of plastic and tin. It was really awful there. It stunk. There was no sanitation and no running water.

The church asked to build a school there, and they wouldn't let us build it because it was a squatter's area. So we just squatted with them and put up a platform with a thatched roof. We had a missionary couple there, and they were teaching reading, writing, arithmetic, and Bible to a platform teeming with children.

The day we were visiting, the teacher told her husband, "Go and find Manuel. He is always here. There's something wrong or Manuel would be here."

Her husband went off and came back with his head down and called her aside and said, "Manuel is dead. His body is lying on a piece of cardboard. I think he died of an abscessed tooth."

Then the mission worker asked her husband what I also wanted to ask, "Why didn't they come to us for help?"

He said, "Well, I asked them that, and the mother said, 'We didn't want to ask you for help because you had already done so much.'"

You know, we have this ridiculous feeling that all people out in the world hate us. The people that our missionaries help do *not* hate us. They love us. They may hate our government, but they don't hate *us*.

As I was standing there in that stinking, rotten place, I made up my mind that I was going to get out into the mission fields and see what we had done. Now I've been out. I raised my own money to go. And as I have gone out, over and over I have found that we have done much, but there isn't any stopping place. There is never a place that we can just say, "Enough."

Once You're There, You're Never Gone

I've said this over and over around the church, "Once you're in a place, once you take the gospel into any country, any location, anywhere, it's never lost, even if you do it wrong." One of the shining examples of that is China.

In the first part of this century, both former Presbyterian denominations spent millions of dollars sending missionaries to China. That was when we had to travel four months on ships and then get in little boats and run up and down the Yangtze River, confusing the Chinese by sending the southern Presbyterians to northern China and the northern Presbyterians to southern China.

But once we were there, what wonderful work we did! We were sent back home on several occasions, and finally, in desperation, all of our mission work was brought home. We stayed just as long as we could, even when Dr. Frank Price was taken prisoner and when many of our missionaries were put under house arrest. Then one of our missionaries was beheaded, and we came home. That was the second time that had happened. In the thirties, one of our missionaries, Jack Vincent, was beheaded in China and his body was dragged through that land by bandits. His church was destroyed. His daughter, who now lives in Aurora, Illinois, says that the church has been rebuilt and now has 2,000 members. Her father was not a martyr in vain.

When we brought all our missionaries home the second time, we wept and we wailed and we gnashed our teeth about all the money and time we had wasted in China. And we didn't just weep and wail that year, we wept and wailed every year. Every time it would come up that we needed money for anything, somebody would eventually get up in a meeting and say, "Oh, oh, oh, if we just hadn't wasted all that money in China. We spent millions of dollars there and now the church is gone."

The church there was never gone. On the very first Sunday it finally went public again, there were 16,000 baptisms. We knew right away there were still a half million Christians in China. It's been twelve years since that Sunday, and there's fifteen million Christians in China today.

I was lucky enough to get to go there soon after it opened up again. I went with Tommy Brown, who had been born there, and many of the early missionaries who wished to return.

The Sunday we were in a crowded church in Beijing, an elderly woman came down the center aisle carrying a box of hymnbooks that she had risked her life to keep hidden for thirty-two years. Would you risk your life to keep hymnbooks hidden?

The hymns in those books were in English and Chinese. We sang through that book for two hours. Imagine how I felt when I turned to the fly page and saw that the hymnbook was printed on Chestnut Street in Philadelphia by the Presbyterian Church.

The next Sunday we were in Shanghai in a former Methodist Church. There were 4,000 people there that day. The communists had knocked out all the stained glass windows in that church, as they had done all over China, because they were symbols of Christianity. But there's something very forceful about a hole in the wall that is shaped like a cross. The people in that church were singing too. They didn't have hymnbooks, but they were singing hymns we had taught them.

And guess what! They remembered the words to the hymns and we didn't. They were singing "In the Sweet By and By." It had been so long since we'd sung that hymn that we couldn't remember the words.

I told the two preachers on either side of me, "We've got to sing anyway. Just make up words and sing anything. They won't know."

Here we were in old Shanghai, and we all looked like nerds. We didn't know the words, but we had to sing anyway. It was wonderful. Nobody cared. I always thought, though, that they picked the next hymn for us, because we sang "Hallelujah, Hallelujah, Hallelujah, Hallelujah." I guess they figured we could get through that one!

You Never Lose It

W e've taken the gospel to many places in the world and even when we've been run out of the country, the church has always remained there. One of those places is Iran, where many of the Christian leaders have been executed or killed in the streets in recent years. But the church has not disappeared from there; the church continues to survive.

I know the church is still alive in Iraq, even though our missionaries were put out of there years ago. When I was in Ann Arbor, Michigan, in a church where there were Iraqi and Iranian Christians, they wept as they left that service because I had said there were Christians in their country. They said nobody had mentioned that in a long, long time.

Cuba, of course, is another example. David Young, who works for the church in Louisville and often goes to Cuba, will tell you about the new enthusiasm for the church in Cuba. One of the reasons for this is that Lois Kroehler, one of our missionaries in Cuba when the revolution began, refused to leave. She stayed there through the entire revolution and remained there until last year when she retired and came back to the States. Even though she has retired, she still goes back and forth to Cuba. She was honored at the Cuban General Assembly for staying with the Cubans, for revising their music, and for the many things that she did for Christians in Cuba.

The church is growing there now, and we have churches from the southeast coast that are helping to build a new Presbyterian church in Cuba. We again have students at the seminary in Cuba, where for many years there was a seminary but no students. There are students again who are studying to be Presbyterian preachers, and the young people have gone back to church. David Young says that when you go to church there, they fill the church up and they sing with great joy. He said they end every service singing "Onward, Christian Soldiers." It's kind of become a battle hymn for them. It's just wonderful to know what's happening to the Presbyterian Church in Cuba.

The last Protestant missionary was put out of Albania when Hitler marched into that country in 1939. Few missionaries had been back there until the University Presbyterian Church in Seattle became interested in that country, and we now have eleven missionaries that they've sent there. The church is alive and well in Albania. You just never lose the church anywhere you take it, no matter what happens.

Do We Go to the Difficult Places?

Many times as I go around the church, people ask me, "Do we go to the difficult places?" I've been to a few places that make me think if there's anywhere more difficult to go, I don't want to hear about it.

One of those is Bangladesh. I don't know how to tell you about it except to say there are no rocks there—not even little rocks. When they need gravel for roads, they have to make bricks out of mud and straw, and little children under six years old sit out in the hot sun with little hammers and break those bricks up for gravel. It saddens my heart to see the child labor there.

I went to Bangladesh and met in their capital with a number of representatives from other denominations, including the Presbyterian Church of Ireland, the Anglican Church of England, and the German Reformed Church.

We were all meeting together with the Christians of Bangladesh to see how we could best help them.

While we were there, a wonderful Anglican sister who has been there forty-two years came up to me and said, "We have a hospital, a school, a church, and agriculture projects, and we really appreciate the Presbyterians giving to them and helping with them."

And I said, "I'm glad to know we do."

She said, "These things are far from the capital, and none of the Presbyterians have ever come to see them."

I answered, "Oh, I'm sure you must be mistaken. I'm sure some Presbyterians have been to see them. I know we have a lot of Presbyterians that come to Bangladesh, and if we're giving to that project, surely some of them have come to see these places."

She repeated, "No, no they have not. But the Archbishop of Canterbury came to see us," she added.

I stood there trying to think of what to say. And she continued, "Would you come? Would you come while you're here?"

I turned to Norman Miller, our missionary there at that time who now oversees our hospital work all over the world, and I said, "Norman, do you think we could go there?"

He said, "Well, I've never been there. Yes, we could try, but you have to give up some of the other things you're doing because of your time pressures."

I said, "If other Presbyterians are seeing some of the other things, maybe we ought to go there."

He said, "All right." He looked a little worried about it, but I thought everything was going to be fine.

The next day we started out in a jeep toward the

Ganghes River. It wasn't all that easy to get there. The traffic was bad and there were bad roads and crowds of people, but I thought, This isn't too bad.

Then we finally got to the Ganghes River, which cuts Bangladesh in half. It comes down from India and cuts right across the country. There's not a single bridge across the Ganghes, not even a little bridge, not even a walking bridge, not even a floating bridge—no bridges at all. No country has donated a bridge to them. Even in China, Russia built a big bridge for them on the Yangtze River, but there are no bridges in Bangladesh.

We got out of our jeep and told it good-by a little reluctantly, hoping it would be there when we came back. Then we got on this old tin boat going across the Ganghes. It was a terrible-looking boat, and they wanted to usher me inside the cabin to let me have a seat. I said, "Oh, no, no, no, I want to stand out here by the railing where I can see the beautiful scenery." What I really wanted was a shot at going over the railing and swimming through that dirty river to shore when the boat went down.

Anyway, we got to the other side. The boat didn't go down, and we got off and there was another jeep. I was very glad to see it, and I asked, "How did we get a jeep over here without a bridge?"

I was told, "Well, we have a couple of jeeps on this side, and we had to go up and bring them all the way down from India."

A lot of times the Presbyterian mission workers have to do things in very difficult ways. We got into the jeep and went off to see our agriculture project. It was exciting to see it. The people knew we were coming. I don't know how Norman got the word around—something about the modern FAX machine. When we got there, they were waiting for me and my traveling companion, Lois Hall from Florida. We were going to be given the opportunity of harvesting the first rice. I knew absolutely nothing about rice. When I was a little child, I picked a little cotton on my grandfather's farm and learned how hard that was, and I pulled a few carrots and hoped that I never had to do that again.

Somebody took a photograph of us down in the ditch, sloshing around in the mud with machetes, cutting rice. After we cut a little bit of rice, the people said, "That's enough."

I think they thought we'd ruin that whole year's crop. So we got out and went to a worship service while they continued to harvest their rice. When we left there, we took off on another road. I thought we'd be at our destination soon, but that wasn't so. We stopped that night at the home of Cindy and Les Morgan, two wonderful Presbyterian missionaries—Johns Hopkins graduates, doctors, both of them. They could be making a fortune in the U.S., but they're out there in Bangladesh with their three children—the only American children for miles and miles and miles there.

The Morgans educate their children and work in two hospitals. We had a wonderful evening with them. We got up early the next morning and started out, and I thought, Well, we'll be there by lunch, because I noticed there was no lunch in the jeep. It was true there was no lunch in the jeep, but that didn't mean we were going to be there by lunchtime because we got lost on the way. We finally got back on the right track, having to travel on a dirt levy and dirt roads. Just as Norman said, "I think we're close now," it started to rain.

I was a little worried about that. Having grown up in flood country in South Texas, I know about dirt levies and dirt roads when it rains. I said to Norman a little uneasily, "You know, I believe the papers you sent us said that if it rains in November, a cyclone may be coming."

"Yes," he said.

I said, "It's November."

"Yes," he said.

I asked, "Do you think a cyclone is coming?"

"Yes," he said.

I said, "We're on dirt roads, and if this is the case, we may not be able to get out of here. We may need to just tell these people we're going to have to see everything very quickly and start right back."

"Yes," he said.

We got to our destination in just a little while and there were little boys from that school standing out in the rain waiting for us with flowers. They gave us flowers and I just wanted to weep at how enthusiastic they were. Little "one-note Charlie," as I called him, got out his bugle. He could only play one note, so he played "toot toot toot, toot toot toot." And another boy whipped up the bass drum with a "boomdy, boomdy, boom," and they paraded us into the school. There wasn't any saying hello and good-by. It wasn't possible. So Norman sent the driver away. And I asked, "How will we get out of here tomorrow?"

He said, "On a little canal; they say they have a little boat."

Wonderful, I thought.

So we stayed. We saw the hospital, and we saw the girls in the school who danced, and we saw the boys march around and do drills. We went to the worship service that night, and we ate supper with the Anglican sisters and then went to bed.

The cyclone was coming and the rats out in the fields knew that. They had moved in as well, so it wasn't a real fun evening because we didn't even want to get up and go to the bathroom for fear of stepping on a rat.

The next day as we left, we got on this skinny little boat in this skinny little canal. I slid down through the mud to get on that boat. They told me to get into the middle of the boat and sit still, and I'll guarantee you I sat very still. But as we started off, I called back to that wonderful Anglican sister and asked how the Archbishop of Canterbury got up there, and she answered, "By helicopter."

Now the Presbyterians couldn't afford a helicopter, so there we were, going out of this narrow, narrow canal in a skinny little boat. I've always been so glad that I ended up going out that way because I saw something that day I wouldn't have seen otherwise. I saw one of the six schools built by One Great Hour of Sharing money.

I took a picture of the school as we went by. It was built on stilts with a flat roof, so it not only served as a school, but it also served as a rescue area when the floods came. And in Bangladesh, every year or so, the floods come.

Doctor Livingston, I Presume

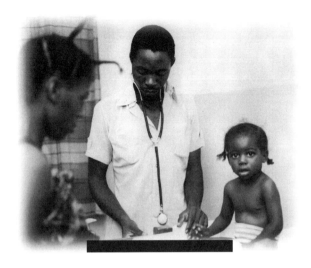

Most people have heard the story about Dr. Livingston. Some of us fail to realize that Dr. Livingston was a Scottish Presbyterian missionary, one of the first ones in Africa. In the area where he settled and did such good work, there is now the Synod of Livingstonia. This area is the present-day country of Malawi, and it is still a wonderful mission area.

One of the stories from there that's really wonderful happened in the fifties. They were having a terrible, terrible time in that part of Africa—a little bit like they've had in Rwanda in recent years. The Scottish missionaries were in great danger. They had a plane fly over from Scotland and drop a canister with a message saying, "If you want to come out, we'll try to get you out some way or another. Please put a big "X" with white rocks and we'll know you want to come out. If you want to stay, put an "I." Well, they put an "I" and then they spelled out "Ephesians." Now if it had been me, I would have used Mark or John or Luke or some shorter name from the Bible. But they spelled out "Ephesians 2:14" with white rocks, and it's still there to remind us of those times.

The Scripture in that verse partially says, "We are all as one," which to them meant that they wanted to stay with their Christian brothers and sisters. *The London Times* ran a picture of that Scripture in the rocks, taken from an airplane, and said in the subtitle, "The Presbyterian missionaries are hearty folks." And they still are hearty — they were then and they are now.

Two of the missionaries there are the Dimmocks. Frank administrates many of our hospitals, working from morning till night, as does his wife. They do good work for us. When I visited there recently, we went to visit our hospitals and our schools. I was so impressed.

Frank also took us up to the place where Dr. Livingston had been. It was a very, very difficult drive. We went up a hill with twenty-three hairpin turns. When he went by to check on the hospital there, he found he had to go right back down in order to save the life of a young Malawi woman. He helped put the patient in the back of the jeep, turned it into an ambulance, and went down to a hospital below that had better facilities. Then he came right back up. He made that trip three times that day, and I was horrified over making it once. Those mission workers are tough.

The only reason we have an ambulance in the area now is because of the Medical Benevolence Foundation, which purchased it. A young man named Mark Anderson, who is a hospital administrator in Milwaukee, flew over to Johannesburg, purchased the ambulance, and drove it up to Malawi. That was the only way we could get it there.

Last year the country had a free election for the first time — something the church had helped call for. We're real proud of that. The churches in Malawi are now full every Sunday.

The doors have to be opened in the back and people stand out on the porch and out in the yard and lean toward the doors so they can hear the message of the preacher and sing songs with the people inside. It's wonderful!

In the Country of Anna and the King of Siam

Many of us are familiar with the story of Anna and the King of Siam because of the play *The King and I.* Very few of us realize that the book on which the play is based was written by Margaret Landon, a Presbyterian missionary who found information for the book in a library when she was serving in Thailand (formerly Siam).

In the book, Anna, the English teacher who came out to teach the king's children, mentioned that the only people in Siam that spoke English were the Presbyterian missionaries. That is because the Presbyterians were the very first to open mission work in that country in the 1850s.

I went to Bangkok and thought that would be where our main mission was. We do have a lot of mission work in Bangkok — a daycare school for poor children, help for the elderly, churches, hospitals, and a wonderful project of trying to get rid of child prostitution in the red light district. I walked through that red light district with Janet Guyer, a very striking young Presbyterian missionary who was born in Thailand and speaks the native language. Her father was a doctor at one of our hospitals.

I thought I had seen our mission work and was going on to another country, but the mission workers said, "Oh, no, no, you must go to Chiang Mai."

And I said, "Where is Chiang Mai?"

They answered, "Nearly up to Burma." They seemed surprised that I didn't know that's where the Presbyterian mission work was.

I asked, "How long have we been up there?"

They answered, "Since the 1850s."

And I asked, "Well, how did we get up there?"

And they said, "By elephant back."

Now that sounds really romantic and fun unless you've done it. I've ridden one elephant and I never intend to ride another. I cannot imagine going all the way to Chiang Mai by elephant back. I went in an airplane and got there not expecting to see a whole lot. Was I surprised!

There was the largest university in the country of Thailand, and it was started by the Presbyterians. There was a wonderful, comparatively new chapel built by the Luce family of *Time* and *Life* magazine fame, who are Presbyterian. And there was the McCormick Hospital there, built originally by money from Cyrus McCormick, who was Presbyterian.

The hospital had been added to in recent years by the Medical Benevolence Foundation. There was a nursing school; there were high schools; there were churches; and over on the island, there was a leprosarium.

The first two missionaries were from North Carolina and Pittsburgh. They worked there for a year and they had only three converts. The King of Siam executed two of the converts because they refused to work for him on Sunday.

That's when I would have gotten on my elephant and gone home. But they stayed, and the two executed converts were considered martyrs. At about that time, the Prince of Siam gave the missionaries an island. A mad elephant had died on the island, and the prince thought it was a place of the devil, so he gave it to the Presbyterian missionaries.

They started a leprosarium there and the church grew. Everywhere we have done work with leprosy victims, the church has grown. We helped leprosy victims in Miraj, India, and the church grew there. We helped leprosy victims in Taiwan and the church grew there. We helped leprosy victims in South Korea and the church grew there.

There's still work on the leprosy island in Chiang Mai, where they build their own wheelchairs and fix their own special shoes. Therapists work with them, trying to help restore the use of their limbs. It's a magnificent work.

There's also a seminary there. We have one seminary professor, Bill Yoder, who's been there thirty years and who treats the students like they're a part of his family. They get married in his house, and their children are like his grandchildren. It's just wonderful to see the good work that's being done in Thailand. It was hard for me to believe that we had that much mission work in this country.

In World War II, we were put out of Thailand because our country was on the other side. The people there hated for the Presbyterian missionaries to leave. Actually, the very last people they asked to leave were the Presbyterians, and the very first ones they asked to come back were the Presbyterian missionaries. That says something about our mission work in Thailand.

Work Along the Border

Mexico is a very interesting mission field that we have been in and out of for years. The border projects are particularly interesting. A lot of our youth workers through the past few years have gone down and helped with border ministry work, all the way from Brownsville, Texas, to San Diego, California, and some of those border projects are really wonderful.

Some of them have had their share of problems, but they always seem to get them worked out. The original project started between El Paso and Juarez a number of years ago. It was originally called Project Verdad.

I remember a Presbyterian pastor from Mexico named Baltizar who started a clinic. When people started coming there, he told them, "We need to start a church."

Everybody that came to the clinic was given a sack

of cement so they could help build a church. He told them to go home and build blocks, using the dirt and the water in their yard. They came back with different-colored blocks. Some were gray, some were brown, some were kind of pink, and some were dirty white. They put them all together and built a church and called it Esperanza, which means "hope." I asked Baltizar about that and he said, "Even the poor must have an opportunity to give, if they love the Lord."

That project has mushroomed all along the border. Years ago the Presbyterian Church of Mexico asked our missionaries and our preachers to go home and leave them alone to do their own work, which we did.

We pulled out and didn't go back until the church started growing in northern Mexico where the border projects were. When the Mexican church realized how fast their church was growing in the north, they invited us back. So today we can work in different places in Mexico, including the Yucatan, where some missionaries stayed to help people even though they weren't under the guise of the Presbyterian Church.

Down in Chiapas, Mexico, where there has been so much trouble, a lot of the Chiapas Indians are Presbyterian because the Presbyterians from Guatemala came and helped bring the Chiapas Indians into the church.

There's one orphanage in Tijuana where retired Presbyterian navy veterans built a lot of the buildings and fences. It's a particularly well-run orphanage. There are many projects in Arizona, in the lower Rio Grande Valley of Texas, and around Del Rio. They're all wonderful ways to show God's love.

And Down in Jamaica

The Presbyterian Church has done a lot of work in Jamaica, mostly in Kingston. They have a seminary, they have schools, and they have many churches.

About six or seven years ago, there was a terrible hurricane and everybody thought the church was completely wiped out. The seminary was blown apart. The roofs were blown off of every single church. The school was almost destroyed. The General Secretary of the Presbyterian Church in Jamaica at that time was Sam Smelly.

When people finally got a call through to Sam, they asked, "Is the church gone down there?"

And Sam told us something we all need to remember. "Of course the church is not gone. The buildings are gone, the roofs are gone, but the church is the people."

The Presbyterian Church (U.S.A.) rallied around Sam and the Presbyterians in Jamaica. I remember that Columbia Seminary in Decatur, Second Presbyterian Church in Louisville, and many other churches around the country helped build those buildings back. As Sam Smelly said, "The church was never gone."

Poor Haiti, Poor Haiti

The Presbyterian Church (U.S.A.) has long tried to help in Haiti. We keep trying and I hope we never give up. We do wonderful work there in a hospital, working alongside the Episcopal Church, which for many years administrated that hospital through a series of doctors. They have stayed through some mighty tough times, including the recent years when we brought all the missionaries out. But the head of the hospital decided he would not leave because he said, "They won't hurt me because we are helping the people."

Outside of that hospital is a well. A faucet runs through the fence where people can come and get good water. The philosophy is that it's better to prevent illness by offering people good water than to put them in the hospital and treat them after they have become sick from bad water.

I went there years ago when they added a new addition to that hospital. I went with Dorothy Bernard, who was then the moderator of the PCUS, and Bill Rice. We arrived in the airport at Port au Prince and it was just a zoo. Everybody was running in every direction, shouting and hollering. The missionaries talked among themselves, and they realized they didn't have enough room at the mission compound for Dotty Bernard and me until the next day, but they didn't tell us. They told the taxi driver where to take us and told Dotty and me to get into the taxi. We thought we were waiting in the taxi for them to go along with us when suddenly the taxi driver took off down the road. Dotty looked at me and asked, "Marj, do you know where we're going?"

And I said, "I don't have the slightest idea, and what's more, we don't have any phone number or address for where the rest of them have gone."

The driver took us to a place called the Hotel Splendid. It was an old hotel that had been stylish in its day and was still a pretty nice place. We got out and enjoyed the evening. We had dinner and listened to a guy at the piano and wondered what in the world we were going to do next.

The next morning the missionaries came and got us and took us to the mission compound near the hospital. We had a wonderful experience there as we went through that hospital. We talked to the Episcopal bishop, met with the board, went through the celebration of increasing and improving that hospital, and realized just how much good the Presbyterians were doing.

I went through the Iron Market in Haiti. People were so desperate because the tourists had quit coming to that country because it was so filthy and raw sewage was running in the streets. As you went through that market the people were so desperate to sell you their wares that they clutched at your arm and pleaded, "Momma, momma please. One dollar buy this. Please, one dollar, momma, please."

To get out of that place, I threw a dollar here and a dollar there. I just bought whatever they were handing me and headed for the exit. My arm was bleeding; I was crying. It was just a terrible experience, and it made me realize more than anything else how really desperate Haitians have become.

Are We in Colombia?

Many times as I have traveled around the church, I have been asked, "Do we do any work in Colombia and South America among the drug barons?" Oh, yes, the Presbyterian Church is in Colombia. Do you remember ten or twelve years back when they had the terrible mud slide there? Do you remember when they showed the awful TV clip of a young teenage girl going down in the mud and nobody could save her? That town was primarily Presbyterian.

We had a hospital, a school, churches, and all kinds of activity there. The whole town went down in the mud slide. The seminary students from there were not at home. They were all in Bogotá attending seminary classes. They lost their families, they lost their homes, but they were more inspired than ever to become pastors and to help their people.

A wealthy woman in Colombia donated some land a few miles from that village and the whole village started over. And so again we have a Presbyterian village there.

Alice Winters, one of our missionaries who's been in South America for a long time, is president of that seminary in Bogotá. She's the only woman who's president of a seminary in all of South America. She does wonderful work and is an inspiration to all those who know her. She has done the most fantastic job of bringing alive the Presbyterian Church in Colombia of anybody who has ever been there.

From the Congo to Zaire

The Presbyterians went into the Congo over a hundred years ago. They went when they had to go down the river in boats, and we used to send supplies into them once a year by boat.

I went to Zaire, which was the former Belgian Congo, in 1983. There was a large group of us and we had to divide into smaller groups because there were too many places to go. John Pritchard was then the associate for the Presbyterian Church for work in Africa, and he was directing who would go where. I remember he asked me, "Marj, where would you like to go?"

I said, "I want to go to Luepo."

He said, "You can't go there. We had a missionary killed there, and we closed that mission field a long time ago. Where do you want to go?"

And I said, "I want to go to Luepo."

"Why?" he said.

I explained, "Because when I was a child in Sunday school, we used to take up pennies and nickels and dimes every Sunday to help buy a new boat to get supplies to the missionaries in Luepo. I think that's where we began our work there. I believe that's where the Sheppards and Lapsleys went. We now have a presbytery named for those two wonderful mission families from Alabama. One was black, one was white, and they went there and started that mission field."

He said, "Well, yeah, that's true."

And I said, "They told us a story about how supplies were brought in on a boat on the Congo once a year. One year the Presbyterians thought they needed a printing press, so they put it on the boat and it sank the boat. Wasn't that a smart thing to do?

"One of the missionaries swam out to try to save the food, not the printing press. He was trying to save the food and he was eaten by a crocodile.

"Now a child will remember that story. I also remember getting home from Sunday school that Sunday and my grandmother asking me, 'Marjorie, what did you learn in Sunday school today?'

"And I said, 'I learned I never want to be a missionary. Crocodiles eat missionaries.' "

Pritchard said, "Oh, for heaven's sake."

And I said, "Well, can I go on a boat down the Congo River like they used to do?"

And he said, "No, they've put a dam in, and there's a big waterfall and that's a problem."

And I said, "Well, yes, that would be a problem. I

don't really want to go over a waterfall."

So I said, "Can I fly in one of those little missionary planes?"

He said, "They don't have a landing strip anymore and that too is a problem."

And I said, "Well, yes, I don't want to go if I can't land. Forget it, I'll go somewhere else."

He said, "No, you've made me mad. I'm going to get you to Luepo, and you're going to be sorry."

So two preachers, Angie Anderton, a missionary who has since died, and I flew to another little village and got in a jeep with a driver and started to Luepo.

We went on very bad roads for quite a while, and finally we stopped at what was solid jungle, which they call "bush." And the driver said, "Now we're going to go on very bad roads."

I thought that's what we had already been doing.

He added, "But don't worry, I am good driver. Let us pray."

We prayed and then we started to Luepo through that bush. Of course there weren't any roads, no roads at all. Years ago when the Belgians were in control of the Congo, they would have the men in each village look after the roads, and they would drive through them with a glass of water on the hood of the car. If the water spilled, they had all the men in that village whipped, claiming the roads were too rough. Naturally, when they got their freedom, the men quit doing any road work.

We did a lot of praying that day. We prayed as we went through the creek beds, praying that an axle wouldn't break. There were no garages there. We prayed as we went through a grass fire with five cans of gasoline in the jeep.

We were absolutely terrified and started beating out sparks. I remember one of the men was crying, and I was saying, "Don't cry. Beat out sparks! Cry later."

But I really was concerned that I had messed up by taking people into Luepo.

When we finally got there, there was a red brick hospital with a doctor we'd trained who was still trying to run it by himself. There were red brick schools. There were red brick gravestones on the graves of our missionaries and their children, and there was a red brick church with a bell and a clock in the tower that was still keeping perfect time.

(I told that story one time in San Antonio in a presbytery meeting, and at the end of my speech, a man jumped up in the back of the church and ran down the aisle. I thought he was getting ready to join the church or something. I didn't know what was going on. He was screaming, "My grandfather put that clock in the tower, my grandfather put that clock in the tower. I can't believe it's still there.")

We rang the bell and everybody came to that church. They filled the church and stood outside all the way to the banks of the Congo River. There was no glass in the windows and you could see this sea of faces. I'm an old cynical reporter and I thought, These aren't all Christians. They just came to see what we're doing here. And then they began to sing the hymns. And every man, woman, and child as far as I could see knew all the words to all the hymns, and I knew again that once the church is in a place, it's never gone. And I wept.

Now Is Not a Good Time

As I go around the church talking about missions, a lot of people in the churches say, "Well, we want to give to missions, and we really believe in missions, but now isn't a good time to give to mission."

They give me all kinds of excuses for that. The crop is bad. If it's a farm area, it either hasn't rained and it's dry or it's rained too much and it's flooded. Or if you're in the oil fields, the oil industry is depressed. Or if you're where there's a big chemical company, the chemical company is having problems. Or there's unemployment where they're building cars. You can go on and on with the excuses.

I got to wondering when the good time was. I thought about it. I was born in 1926. Of course that was the time when they were bootlegging whiskey and the Mafia was getting going. I don't remember it, but I know it wasn't a good time.

But I do remember the Depression that followed. I remember my mother giving bread and butter and jam sandwiches to people who came to our door. That's all we had extra to give. That sure wasn't a good time.

Then we had World War II, and although a lot of young people like to think of that as a wonderful patriotic war, those of us who lived through it know it was just another rotten war where our relatives and friends were killed. And it wasn't a good time.

After that war, we built a big bomb and we were afraid somebody else might have one too. For a while we all went to church. Those were the best churchgoing years we had. But nobody dropped a bomb on us so we quit going to church. Then we had the Korean conflict and that wasn't a good time. After that we had the sixties. We had all the demonstrations and confusion on our campuses and that wasn't a good time. We had the Vietnam conflict and that sure wasn't a good time. We had the Gulf War and that wasn't a good time. And so I've been wondering when this good time is coming.

I wondered how I was going to respond to people who said, "Now isn't a good time to give to missions," and I finally found out. In 1989, the members of the Presbyterian church of Cameroon invited me to come to their 125th anniversary, and I went. It was a difficult trip because I was talking up in Hudson River Presbytery in a snowstorm. When I left Kennedy Airport it was 18°, and when I got to Cameroon, it was 118°. That's a hundred degree difference and it can wilt you fast.

But we had a wonderful week. They were really celebrating there. They had parades and were on television. They had concerts. They had worship services and banquets.

It was just a marvelous week. Then on Sunday there were so many people that they had to hold the celebration outside. They put the altar outside of the church and 40,000 Cameroon Presbyterians sat up on the hillside. Eight choirs sang and they rattled things and played drums and danced around. It was a great event.

Finally it got quiet and there was just a single drum with a single beat in the background. I looked up to see what was happening, and I saw a long line of Cameroon Presbyterian preachers processing in one by one, and they were singing in French. I don't speak French, but I knew they were singing, "The Church's One Foundation Is Jesus Christ Our Lord." I knew we had done something right in Cameroon.

As I flew back home, I thought about what I'd experienced. I was so happy about it and was feeling good. Then I took a pencil and subtracted and I got 1864. I thought, No way could we have started a mission field in 1864. Now you talk about a time that wasn't a good time — that's when Presbyterians were killing Presbyterians and brothers were killing brothers in this country. It was the worst time in the history of our land.

When I got back home, I asked for the key to the churches' record room, and I went to look up the minutes of the General Assembly of 1864. I found what I was looking for under "Foreign Missions Report." It said, "The world is watching us in our travail to see if we're serious about the global mission and the Great Commission." It named the first three missionaries that were opening a mission field in the Cameroons. (It was plural then, French and English Cameroon.)

and English Cameroon.)

I sat there quietly for a long time and finally pulled down the minutes of the "Presbyterian Church of the Confederacy," which is what the Southern Church called themselves at that time. Under "Foreign Missions Report" it said, "Our backs are to the wall and our homes are being burned and our churches destroyed, but we must send another missionary to Brazil." It named that missionary.

Now those four missionaries were sent out at greater sacrifice than anything we have done in a long, long time. It was the worst of times in the history of our country. So I don't want to hear the words "Now is not a good time."

How Did We Do That?

We would like to bring the church above ground in North Korea, like what has happened in China. At this time in North Korea, there is one Protestant and one Catholic church and they are full every Sunday. But we know we have at least 500 congregations underground there, and there is nothing we can do about it at this time.

Insik Kim and Syngman Rhee have visited in North Korea, and they have spoken to the older dictator there, who had admitted to them that when he was a little boy, he went to a Presbyterian Sunday School. He recently died and his son is in charge, and his son has no Christian history whatsoever. We have to pray for North Korea.

South Korea, on the other hand, blows our mind. The Young Nak Presbyterian Church in Seoul has 60,000 members. They have six or seven services every Sunday, with the first one at 6 A.M. When you come out of church, six or seven thousand people are in the foyer or in the yard and almost out in the street waiting to go to church. How did we do that? Is it the only church in town? That's not so because crosses rise all over that city and all over that country.

South Korea is the only Christian nation in Asia, and the largest denomination there is Presbyterian. How did we do that? The Presbyterian Church in South Korea is sending out 400 missionaries of their own. How did we do that?

Of course we had good missionaries there, but we have good missionaries everywhere. The church grows wherever God decides it will grow, and that's where God decided it would grow. I think another reason the church has grown there is that we stood with the Koreans when they were persecuted. When you stand with people when they are persecuted, the church grows every time.

When an army of occupation controlled that country, we stood with them. And when the army tried to walk the leprosy victims into the sea by moving them from the center of Korea to the south, Dr. Robert Wilson went with them and carried them. That was in a time when you thought that if you touched leprosy, you got it.

The church bought the land in the very southern part of South Korea and put up a leprosarium and the church grew. Later when leprosy victims could be cured but could not go back into society, we gave them little plots of land where they had gardens, and raised chickens, and built a church out of rocks.

I went to that church one Sunday with Clarence and Ruth Durham, who were missionaries there. Everybody else there was a leprosy victim. Four blind leprosy victims came to the front of that church and played hymns on harmonicas. God was in that church. Maybe that is why we grew in South Korea.

When I was staying with missionary friends in South Korea, I woke up one morning and heard all this racket. I jumped out of bed and asked what it was all about. The hosts said, "It's the church elders standing on the church roof of the Presbyterian church down the hill, singing hymns to greet the day."

I said, "Are you sure they're Presbyterians?" That enthusiasm just overwhelmed me.

I've been to Korea several times, and every time I go, I am impressed with the people's dedication and their ability to do evangelism because they do it one-on-one. They talk to their friends and neighbors and people they work with, and they invite them all to come and learn about Jesus Christ. It is absolutely amazing. Our church would grow if we did that.

Where Is Dourados?

W here in the world is Dourados? It's part of Brazil, but it's not a part of Brazil that we usually think about. It's down near the border of Paraguay. It's more like West Texas than the parts of Brazil that we usually think about, such as the Amazon. It's just desolate there, and there are a lot of sandstorms. Many native peoples live there.

The Presbyterian Church has served there for a number of years and has served very carefully. At one time, the Methodist mission was put out of Dourados by the government because people said the mission was interfering with their culture and trying to change it. We have tried very hard not to do that.

We have a seminary there, a school for children, and two hospitals, one of which is a tubercular hospital because there's so much tuberculosis in that area. There's also a big church, and it's very, very active.

All of these things that the Presbyterians have are outside the actual area where the indigenous people live. I think the government has let us stay because we were not inside their living territory trying to change the way they live.

The school children are really the hope for that part of the world. When we visited, they sang Christian songs and their faces were bright and happy. The children who acted as extras in the movie *The Mission* were our school children. They played the part of the children of that time.

The area we visited was very desolate. One of the sad things was that they still used wood for cooking and there was never much wood in that area. It was a prairie area, and they have just used up all their wood. The missionaries told me that every time they go in, they try to take a pick-up load of wood, because the people need wood as much as they need anything else.

The people were poor and usually barefoot, and there was a heavy drinking problem among the male population. The women looked particularly desperate. Some of the little children would run away from us when we came in because they had heard bad stories about white people being demons. But when we would go in with our missionary, children would rush to her. Mothers would hand her their babies to hold, and she would talk to the women. It was rewarding to see what an impact the Presbyterian mission work had in Dourados.

And Up in the Amazon

Dourados is one part of Brazil. The Amazon is another. They're as different as the Dead Sea is from the Himalayan Mountains. It's just incredible.

The Amazon is a lush jungle with huge rivers running through it. Thus, the areas are often flooded. Bob Cowser, one of our missionaries there, had learned how to build churches that could withstand the flood.

They would build them on a slope with concrete floors and cinder tile blocks, and they would bolt the pews down. When a flood was coming, they would take out all the hymnbooks, Bibles, and everything else they could, open the doors and windows, and let the water rush on through. Later they would have to go back and clean up the mud, but they still had a building. It was an amazing thing to see.

The Amazon highway there was originally started by the women's Presbyterian Birthday Offering. I had always thought I would get there and see a great big highway because I thought that was what I'd given money to build. Instead, it's a long, two-lane red-dirt road into nowhere, but it does get the people and our missionaries to where they worship.

I went with Bob and Sue Cowser one Sunday, and they stopped at ten or twelve locations where they conducted a worship service. I was absolutely amazed at attending ten or twelve worship services on one Sunday. While we were in the jeep, we ran over a huge snake. I remember it was a pretty snake, but I don't like snakes. I asked Bob if there were many of those up there and he said, "Oh, yes."

Right after that he turned into the jungle (or the bush), went up the hill, and stopped, and I asked, "What are we doing?"

He said, "Well, we're going to get out and have church."

And I asked, "Outside?"

He said, "Yes."

These people brought benches out of their homes and sat them up under the trees and we had church. I was still worried about that snake, and I wasn't in a very worshipful mood.

Sue Cowser played the call to worship on the flute. I had always heard that snakes liked flutes, so it was not a particularly wonderful moment to me. I was looking around hither and thither and worrying about the whole situation. But it turned out to be a good worship service for me when I finally got my mind around it and realized that these people counted on the church coming to them on Sunday.

Another time I was in the Amazon, we stopped at the home of a Presbyterian elder. He had killed a deer and was going to serve us a very fancy lunch. We were all standing around in his home talking and visiting, and the rains came. There was a tin roof on his home and when the rains hit that tin roof, the conversation was over. There were no window screens on the windows and suddenly that room was filled with butterflies. The most beautiful butterflies in the world are in that jungle in the Amazon. And here was a room full of wonderful, beautiful orange and black and blue and green and purple and pink butterflies.

I remember standing there thinking that my grandmother was the one who interested me in missions, and somehow I hoped she could see me there in the Amazon in that elder's home, with the rain pouring down on the tin roof, and venison on the table, and the room filled with butterflies. To me, it was a real sign of God's love for the whole world.

Do We Ever Work Well with the Catholics?

Sometimes I'm asked if we work in cooperation with the Catholics in any part of the world. Some places we do and some places we don't.

In Chile, before Pennochet was voted out of power, our preachers there were actually in danger of being arrested. We were already trying to figure out a way to get them out in a kind of underground railroad system and bring them to the United States for additional education. We were going to do this to keep them from going to jail because they had been very vocal in opposing the dictatorship there.

Guess who saved them? It was a Catholic Cardinal who took up for them. The Catholic Church was strong there, and when they took up for our Presbyterian preachers, it became safe for them to stay.

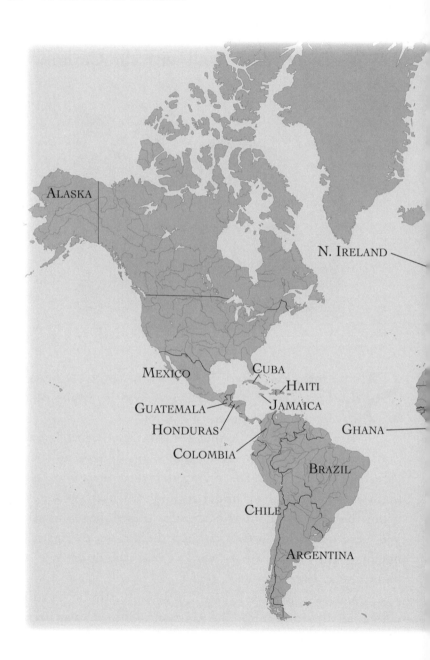

I went to Chile the year that was happening, and the churches there were quite distressed that they were having to do so many things in secret. I remember we had to drive until nearly midnight once to talk to a session that wanted to talk to us at night so that no one would notice that they were talking to us.

I thought, however, it was pretty obvious that something was happening when we drove up in this little jeep van and saw the session members leaning against the church building at midnight, trying to look casual in their shirts and ties. I thought anyone could figure out they were getting ready to have a session meeting.

We went in and talked to them and had a wonderful evening. Even though it was the end of a long day and we were all tired, we suddenly came alive again as we heard about the church and what it was doing in Chile.

We also went to a church service in a home in an area where there was no church building. When they started the worship service, the neighbors came from everywhere and children came from everywhere, and it was really an experience to worship with those Chilean people right in their backyard.

And in Argentina?

Right next door is Argentina, and that is not a country where we work well with the Roman Catholic Church. The Catholic Church is very strong there and very decisive about wanting to do its own thing and have everybody else leave it alone.

We have had a kind of mixed history in Argentina. In Buenos Aires there are two Presbyterian churches. One of them was built years ago by the Church of Scotland. It's a gorgeous old church and looks very Scottish-Presbyterian inside. It nearly ran itself out of business by refusing to have any service that wasn't in English. Just in the last ten years they've added a Spanish service, and finally that church is coming alive.

They also have an ecumenical project there working with young unmarried mothers who are out of work and living on the streets. They give them jobs folding plastic trash bags. It's a job the young girls can do at a place they can stay until their baby is two months old. This at least gets them on their feet a little before they have to go out into nothing again. I worry about where they go afterwards, but at least the babies get a healthier start.

The other church we had there was very active and had three services—one in English, one in Spanish, and one in Taiwanese. As one group would leave, another group would come in. How wonderful to have a church that can serve that many different kinds of people on any given Sabbath! Unfortunately, on the fence near the church, people had painted swastikas and ugly remarks about the church because of the antagonism between the Catholics and Protestants in Buenos Aires.

One of our missionaries there went every Wednesday to walk with the mothers who had lost their children during that terrible time in Argentina when so many people just disappeared. The mothers still go every Wednesday and walk in front of the Pink House, which is the same as our White House. They walk in an orderly manner in a circle, carrying pictures of those children that they've never seen again and little signs asking, "What happened to our children?" One of our missionaries walked with them every week for many, many years. I believe that missionary is now retired, but I think those mothers are still walking. They don't make any commotion, they don't cause a riot, they don't make a lot of noise—they simply keep that reminder out there.

Are We in Ireland?

Many Presbyterians ask, "Is there anything we can do to help in Ireland?" Presbyterians have mixed opinions on what's happening in Northern Ireland. The one thing I learned in visiting Northern Ireland is that when you say you don't understand what's going on there, you've come a long way toward understanding things better. I'm not sure the people there understand either. They simply talk about "the troubles."

Those people have the longest memories of any people I have ever seen. They remember everything that's happened in Ireland for the past 900 years. It's one of the places in the world where Christians battle with Christians, which always makes me particularly sad. What is wonderful there is that the Protestant and the Catholic churches are full every Sunday. But they still have never gotten together.

I don't know where the point of contact is going to be. They don't live in the same part of town, they don't work together, they don't go to church together, they don't read the same newspapers, they don't sing the same songs, they don't play the same sports—there's absolutely no point of contact. Schools may be the key. On the whole, they don't go to the same schools, and one of the things we have tried to do is to start integrated schools—Protestants and Catholics going to school together.

I went to a tree-planting ceremony at one of those schools. I believe Chuck Hammond and Ken Hall helped plant the tree that day. We all stood around and talked to the teachers, and then a young pastor from Butler, Pennsylvania, went over to talk to a little boy. He asked the little boy, "Are you going to go to this school?"

"Yes," the little boy said.

"Are you Catholic?" asked the pastor.

"No."

"Then you're Protestant."

"No, I'm atheist."

And the pastor asked, "What is an atheist, son?"

The lad replied, "My momma says that if you're an atheist, you don't get killed by either side."

Now it's frightening to think that children are starting to think that way in Northern Ireland. The churches are full every Sunday, but they're not going to be for long if the children and young people are starting to think like that.

We have a camp up at Corrymeela, which is one of the most beautiful spots in the whole world. At that camp a Catholic priest and a Protestant preacher can talk to each other without being in danger of losing their lives. It's a place where a family that is intermarried between Catholic and Protestant can go in the summer to get a little bit of rest and relief from the pressures they live under. It's a wonderful place and it's run by our missionaries, the Bakers.

We also are trying to work through our Presbyterian Foundation with Ireland, trying to help provide jobs and help with the economy. Joe Beeman, who is now in New Zealand as Ambassador, started that work, and it is now being carried on by Hank Postel, a pastor from the Washington, D.C., area. The Presbyterian Women provided a Thank Offering Project there a few years back where they had a daycare center on the peace line.

The walls are not down in Belfast. We tend to think that when the wall went down in Berlin, all the walls were down in the world, but the wall is still not down in Belfast.

We Can't Feed the Whole World

How often I've heard the statement "We can't feed the whole world." No, we can't feed the whole world, but when there are children and adults starving to death and we have so much, we have to try to help.

I used to be a little selfish in my thinking about that. And then in late 1984, I went along with the hunger committee to Ethiopia. That was the year they were having their terrible famine. The BBC brought it to the attention of the whole world by showing those children in such desperate straits. We were in shock.

Presbyterians, seeing the results of that hunger, gave eight million dollars to help. Then they got worried because some of the reporters were saying that the food wasn't getting there. I've been a reporter most of my life, and if I made a statement like that, I'd want to be very sure about it. The problem was that the reporters weren't there. They were back here reporting on heresay about what was happening there.

We went into the area where they were distributing food, and we saw that the food *was* getting there. We had learned in Cambodia that if you just distribute food randomly, the people that are hungry will build a community around that food distribution center and never leave.

They didn't do it this way in Ethiopia. They issued food to people to take back to their villages. I'll never forget the sight of all of those starving people sitting on the hillside. Some of them were so weak they couldn't knock the flies off their faces. It was a horrible sight. They didn't push and shove trying to get to the food. Their village leaders told them who was next.

There were volunteer nurses from all over the world who came and helped with that project. They lived in tents in really bad circumstances to help a few months, and then they were relieved by other nurses who would help a few months. A lot of them, interestingly enough, were from Ireland. Irish people grew up on the stories of the potato famine, and they understand famine better than we do in this country.

I stood in a cavelike room full of young mothers, and children, and babies. They had given the young mothers orange cups of powdered milk to drink while they were telling them how they were going to issue food to them to take back to their villages. They told them they were going to weigh and measure their children and that when they came back for more food, they would weigh and measure them again and see if they were doing better.

I stood there and wondered why I was so bothered. As a reporter I had covered murder scenes, train wrecks, plane crashes, car accidents, and a lot of other terrible things, and yet I was weeping. I finally realized that it was because of the silence. There is nothing in God's world more terrible than a room full of babies too weak to cry, babies so weak they only make mewing sounds. I was horrified when I saw a child die just a few feet away because of being just a little too late to get food.

I took pictures of the boxes of food from Church World Service that were there, and I took pictures of food from the United States Government Relief that was there. I wanted people to know that the food was getting there. I felt good about the Presbyterian missionaries who were helping and the Presbyterian food that was there.

Some of the missionaries there now are children of former missionaries that were there, such as Harold Kurtz, who's so active in Frontier Fellowship. His children are now working in Ethiopia. "Mish kids" are some of the best missionaries in the world because they don't have to go through culture shock. They've been born in these countries and they know about them and understand them, and they love the people there. I really believe that second-, third-, and fourth-generation missionaries are some of the best we have. That may be one of the reasons we've succeeded so well in areas like South Korea, where I understand we had even five generations of some families that did mission work in that land. It's really rewarding to see family after family go back and try to help again, even as the mission work changes. As the world changes, the Church of Jesus Christ and the Presbyterian family is always there.

One of the biggest problems now is in southern Sudan where Presbyterians keep starving, and starving, and starving. They had a war going on for ten years and were cut off in the southern part of the country. The northern part of the country and the government of the country is Muslim. I don't think they're the least bit interested in protecting or saving the Christians in southern Sudan. We seem to keep forgetting them as well. Four years ago they had an Easter service with 10,000 Presbyterians sitting outside, and at the end of the Easter service, they picked up ten bodies of Sudanese Presbyterians who had starved to death during the service.

When we heard that, we got to feeling guilty and became interested in helping and sent support for a little while. But interest fades out. I don't know what the answer to that is. Bill Lowry came home from being a missionary in Africa and has been working out of our Washington office trying to help keep the United States government aware of what is happening in Sudan. But of course there are so many other problems that the government considers more important than that. We worry a lot about what to do in the former Yugoslavia. We worry about Rwanda, and we should, but everybody seems to forget about Sudan.

Ironically, we also have Presbyterians that would like to build a big wall around this country and not help anybody, but we have passed the point where we can do that. We have invented airplanes and bombs and telephones and FAX machines and televisions and word processors and all these wonderful things that tie us all together and keep us from being apart again. There is no way to isolate ourselves from the world. Instead, we must learn to live in and love the world.

And the Mamma Dancers Welcome Us

Have you ever heard of the "mamma dancers" in Africa? They're just wonderful. We saw them in Malawi and we saw them in Ghana. When you go into a village where they have a group of "mamma dancers," these women come up in their long colorful cotton dresses with their cotton turbans tied around their heads and they began to dance and sing and sway. It is just one of the most marvelous welcomes you can have anywhere.

In Malawi this happened to us as we went into an area where we have done some agriculture development and worked with a school and a church. I just wanted to weep with joy when I saw these people who were joyful under very poor circumstances.

When I went to Ghana one time, they did a "mamma dance" where they got in a long line and swayed around, singing and dipping and coming back up. Each "mamma dancer" held a handkerchief, and as they dipped and swayed out there in the bush in Ghana, I thought it was one of the most beautiful ballets I'd ever seen anywhere. The next time I went to Ghana, I took every handkerchief I could find in my old dresser drawer. You never saw so much joy over anything in your life.

I think Christians here could learn a lot about music from our Christian sisters and brothers in some of these countries because they sing a lot livelier than we do.

In Cameroon, the women of the church did a wonderful drama acting out the history of when the missionaries came. The women wore men's topcoats and ties and hats straight on their heads and carried Bibles under their arms. They marched in, turning at right angles and singing the old traditional hymns from America and Europe. It was funny to watch. Then suddenly they burst into the more joyful songs they sing today. Music is a special force, and sometimes it ties us all together.

On a trip into Hungary, a group of us went out to a senior citizens home where we were to have lunch. We weren't doing well at all there in relating to the people. We didn't speak the same language, and they stood way back against the wall glaring at us. When we went in to eat, we had the feeling that they just thought we were eating up their food and were there for nothing else. After lunch, we sadly went back into the foyer and were standing around trying to decide what to do.

Then, bless her heart, Dr. Melva Costen from Atlanta sat down at the piano and began to play. The people from Hungary began to creep away from the walls. I remember saying to her, "Play the old Reformed hymns,

Melva. They have a Reformed Church background." And she played some of those wonderful old Reformed hymns, such as "A Mighty Fortress Is Our God" and "Faith of Our Fathers," and one elderly woman (who must have been in her nineties) stepped forward and in a quavering voice, began to sing the hymn in her language. When the next hymn started, we all began singing. They sang in Hungarian and we sang in English. Suddenly we were all hugging each other and crying. When we went to the bus, one woman hurried up to her room and came down with little cards with Scriptures on them in Hungarian and little butterflies and flowers painted on them. She gave us each one. She had made them for special gifts. And suddenly we knew we were all one church—we all loved the Lord. Music, sometimes, is a wonderful key.

The Church Is Still the Light of the World

B ack in 1983 I went with a group of twenty-two people to Ghana. At the time Ghana was having a famine. Now twenty-two Presbyterians can eat a country out of house and home in two weeks, so John Pritchard, who was then associate for our work in Africa, suggested that we each take a footlocker of food.

We divided up the food. Some took rice, some took beans, some took powdered milk, and some took powdered eggs. We knew we were going to have trouble getting the food into that country because the people would think it was black market and we were trying to sell it. They weren't accustomed to people bringing in food to give away.

We got to Ghana and as we were about to check into customs, Pritchard suggested that I take all the footlockers through. I said, "You have to be kidding. You're going to get me arrested."

He said, "Oh, you'll think of something. You always get through customs easily. You look like somebody's grandmother about to have a heart attack. Why don't you give it a try?"

I went out and looked around customs, and I picked a kindly looking gentleman and got into that line. Well, he left the checkpoint and an angry-looking young woman took over. I thought, Oh dear, I am in trouble now.

I never will forget how the young woman shouted at me as she opened the first trunk. "Who are you, and what are you doing here?" she screamed.

I was holding out my passport with it open to my picture, and I was saying, "I am Marj Carpenter from Atlanta, Georgia."

She never let me get any further. She screamed at me again, "No. Who are you and what are you doing here?"

I closed my passport and said simply, "I am here with the Presbyterian Church of the United States, and I have come with gifts for our friends, the Presbyterian Church of Ghana."

She suddenly got a big smile on her face and said, "I went to a Presbyterian Girl's School." I never was so glad to see a Presbyterian kid in all of my life. She looked around quietly and said, "Is there food in all of these?"

I answered, "Yes."

She said, "People kill for that much food in Ghana. You must hire a guard immediately." She said, "I will send your trunks through, but you must hire a guard."

I went running back to tell Pritchard, "They're going to let us through, but they're going to kill us all if you don't get guards for that food."

He found a truck, hired two guards, and sent the food on its way.

Some of our Christian brothers and sisters then came along and put us in a tired old van. After it broke down three times, I started keeping track, and before we got there, it broke down thirty-seven times. The military stopped us three times and told us if we were not off the road by midnight, we were all going to see the Ghana jail.

It was a horrible trip. It was hot. Some in the group were crying. You could hear the jungle sounds. It was just awful.

We finally got to where we were going, a girl's school. I wondered if it were the same one that the customs worker had attended. It was ten minutes till midnight when we arrived, so they immediately sent the men across the road to the dormitory. The two women clergy and I were sent upstairs in an old building built by the Church of Scotland, with winding stairs, no electricity, and no plumbing.

We were banging along trying to get upstairs with our bags, and we came to a kerosene lantern on the landing. We took it with us and let it burn down in the night. It was kind of comforting to Mary Jane Winter, JoAnna Adams, and me. I remember the last thing JoAnna said that night. I had just said, "I have been to worse places."

And she said, "Marj, you're a liar."

The next day we were driving around downtown and saw this line about eight blocks long. I asked, "What are they waiting for?"

Lines fascinate me. In this country we wait in line in amusement parks, rock concerts, football games, Superbowls, and World Series. In Korea, they wait in line to go to church. In Sudan and Somalia and parts of Russia, they wait in line for food. And in Ghana, they were waiting in line for kerosene. I felt terrible because I thought about the fact that some woman had stood in line all day long so that these three American women could get upstairs and go to bed. It bothered me.

But that lamp has become a symbol of the church to me. It wasn't much light but it was very comforting that night. The church is still the light of the world. Sometimes it's not much light, but it's better than no light at all, and it's very comforting to know it's out there. It's put out there at great sacrifice by somebody and it's refueled later on at great sacrifice by somebody. We're all glad to know that the Church of Jesus Christ is still the light of the world.

What Are We Doing in Russia?

M any people ask, "What are we doing in Russia?" We have some kind of misbegotten idea that we need to rush into Russia and take Jesus to the former communists. The interesting thing about the Eastern churches and the churches in Russia is that they never did lose Jesus. They had better attendance than the Western European churches, which were wide open and free.

One of the times I went into Russia was when it was still very communist. It was shocking to see how closely people who attended church were watched.

We went to an old monastery there and everybody was going to climb up in a clock tower to see this old clock. They loved to show us things like old clocks, old churches, old museums, and old everything, just as people do all over the world. I was absolutely at the end of my day and could not climb up into a clock tower, so I told them I'd wait out on the park bench.

I sat down to wait and I noticed people coming out of a church in the middle of the week. I was so impressed I started taking pictures of them coming out. Then I suddenly noticed a man glaring at me.

I put my camera down and wondered what I had done wrong. The man went in the church and came back out with the priest, who came over to me and began talking to me in Russian. I told him, "English, English, American, American." And then he spoke in English. He had been to the World Council of Chruches in Vancouver as one of the representatives.

He asked me why I was taking pictures and I told him. He said, "Well, it's all right. We were afraid you were KGB." Then he explained that these people were at a funeral service. I was really embarrassed and began to apologize profusely. Then he said, "The people don't always go to church because it sometimes costs them their jobs or their apartments. But they had come to this funeral service and were afraid you were taking pictures of them so someone could take their jobs or their apartments away from them."

I was really feeling bad by then. The priest must have sensed this and he asked me in for tea. In the meantime, our group came down from the clock tower, and the guide for the Russian tourist agency was hunting everywhere for me. When she found me, she was very distressed and wanted to know where I'd been. I said, "Oh, I just got lost wandering around." I didn't want to involve that poor priest.

On another occasion on that same trip, we were in a village in the country outside of Moscow, and our tourist guide told us with great pride as she pointed to a bell tower with nine bells, "Those are some of the most beautiful bells in all of Europe."

I said, "Can we hear them?"

"Never on Wednesday," she said.

I turned to our group and said, "And if we were here on Thursday, it would be never on Thursday; if we were here on Friday, it would be never on Friday."

This made her angry and she marched off and came back with an elderly bell ringer. I could see he was quite excited, and I had the feeling that he hardly ever got to ring those bells. They sent him up to the bell tower. With so many bells, there should have been several bell ringers, but this one man was running around up there ringing all the bells. Birds flew out because they had nests in those bells. It was obvious that the bells had not been rung in a long time. People who were hoeing in the fields stopped work and looked up when they heard the bells, so we knew they were seldom rung.

I taped those bells and we played the tape for the bell ringer later, and he had the most joyful look on his face.

I will never forget that we got to hear the bells. My hope is now that Russia is so much freer than it used to be, that they can hear their own bells, which really are some of the most beautiful in the world.

Yes, we're working in Russia. We have our Alaskan Presbyterians helping in Siberia. We have Korean American Presbyterians from Los Angeles helping in an area up near the border of China where some of the

Koreans fled in the North Korean war and had been without a church until we got a missionary in there. We're helping with an eye doctor in a place where we were invited. Our peace office sent Bibles to be distributed by the American Baptist Church.

We are working in Russia and we are very careful in places where we're needed and wanted, in places where there is no Christian church. We're not trying to compete with the Russian Orthodox Church because that's the church that kept Christianity alive behind the Iron Curtain.

Those grandmothers, those "Babushkas," slipped into the church at night and had their grandchildren baptized. They went to Easter services from 1:00–4:00 A.M. because it wasn't a public holiday, but they still wanted to celebrate that Christ is risen. Yes, Christ is risen indeed!

Why Don't We Help in Rwanda?

Anytime Presbyterians hear on the news there's a disaster in the world, they expect the church to respond immediately, and the church does respond just as quickly as it can.

One of the ways we respond is through our World Service Office. That office responded very quickly to the Oklahoma City disaster, the earthquake in California, Hurricane Andrew in Florida, and the flood area in Middle America and South Georgia. They also respond to disaster around the world. And of course we have responded to Rwanda!

Our African office is in very close contact with the people in the refugee areas there. The Presbyterian church in Rwanda was strong, and we had turned it over to the people there, just as we try to do everywhere.

Two weeks before that terrible disaster in Rwanda, Susan Ryan had been there trying to determine a way to get more money for food for the children in the Presbyterian schools. She had talked to a young woman there and worked out how to do that. Three weeks later, she found out that young woman was dead. There was just absolute chaos there.

Jon Chapman, who is one of our present associates to Africa, along with a former Zairian Presbyterian, went into the refugee area in Rwanda to help determine what we can do there to help. They found over a hundred Presbyterian preachers in the refugee camps.

We are planning to go back and help them rebuild the Presbyterian Church of Rwanda. We just have to be very careful about when. We don't want to go back in and rebuild it and have it destroyed again immediately. We are in very close contact with the people there, and we intend to continue to work there. The Rwandan Presbyterian Church will return!

Neighbors Help Neighbors

A few years ago I was able to go to Barrow, Alaska, which is not the beauty spot of the world. But neither is Big Spring, Texas, where I live. However, the people are wonderful in both places.

A lot of Alaska is just absolutely gorgeous. However, you reach a point where you go beyond the forest and the mountains and the streams, and you go on up to the top and that's where Barrow is located. I understand there was somebody from San Antonio, Texas, up there running a Mexican restaurant, which he called "North of the Border." I guarantee you that's as north of the border as you can get.

There's not a road in or out of Barrow. You might remember that Will Rogers and Wally Post died in an airplane crash flying into Barrow. It was a young Presbyterian elder who found that crash.

For a period of two weeks in August, they bring ice breakers into the Arctic Ocean and break up the ice so they're able to bring in barges with supplies.

If you buy a car in Barrow, you get it in August. You don't get one at any other time. If you want lumber for the school or for your home, it comes in August. I know our preachers up there get most of their groceries in August on that barge. All the rest have to be flown in very expensively.

Barrow is not a pretty town. The ground is frozen all year so there are no trees. There are no flowers and there's no grass. I wrote my children a postcard from there that said, "This is not the end of the world, but you can see it from here." It really is a desolate area. But right in the middle of that town is a big green Presbyterian church and it is the heart of Barrow. That church is there because Sheldon Jackson went up there 108 years ago by dogsled and started a church. Now, nearly everybody in Barrow is Presbyterian.

I went to their church on Sunday. I preached twice, I went to Sunday School, I came back and preached that night. I was ready to go over to the manse and hang a blanket on the window, because it's light all night in August, and try to go to sleep. But the people said, "No, no, no, you must stay and hear our radio broadcast."

I asked, "What radio broadcast is that?"

"Well," they said, "every Sunday night we do a radio broadcast and we send it down to Nome, and Nome has a facility to send it around the top of the world. So it goes around to Lapland and Greenland and Siberia."

I was fascinated with that, and I asked, "What do you do on the program?"

I found out they have a blackboard for everybody who wants to be on the program to sign their name on.

They had Bible stories, and Scripture, and hymns. They asked me to tell the story of the boat in Zaire being sunk as they took the supplies into the missionaries once a year. The people in Barrow understood that story since they only got their supplies once a year.

At the end of the program the people rushed up to the microphone and sang "Jesus Loves Me" in their native language.

When the wall went down in Berlin and then the walls began to go down in Russia so that you could get across the Bering Sea again, the Barrow Presbyterians began to work with their presbytery and synod to get over to Siberia to try to start churches where there were no churches at all.

Many Presbyterians think the gospel has already been taken into all the world and there are no new places to go. But in Siberia there were no churches, not even Russian Orthodox Churches.

As the Barrow Presbyterians went up to their sisters and brothers there in Siberia, the Siberians sang to them, "Jesus loves me this I know for the Bible tells me so."

They asked them, "Where did you hear that?"

And the people said, "On the radio."

Oh, the Barrow Alaskans were proud! But then one of the Siberians stepped forward and asked, "Have you come to tell us who this Jesus is that loves us?"

We think we've been into all the world, and that area is only eighteen miles from the United States!

Did You Ever Go to Cuba?

In 1985 I was lucky enough to go to Cuba to a meeting of the North American and Caribbean Council of the World Alliance of Reformed Churches. It was just marvelous to get to go there.

I observed a funny incident while waiting in the Miami airport. I watched Cubans boarding a charter plane. Many of them were trying to take gifts and other things to their relatives in Havana. The airlines official told one woman she had way too much weight in her luggage. She went behind a post and opened her suitcase. She took the boots out, and put them on her feet; she put five or six coats and sweaters on, and went back and weighed the luggage. This time it was all right. All the weight was then on her instead of in the luggage. I laughed a lot about that.

We flew into Havana and for some reason, I got through customs very quickly. I think it was because I had a little tape player, and the customs officials played it to see what it was. It was right after Christmas and the tape was of my children singing Christmas carols. The official thought it was just wonderful, and she sent me right on through the line.

I got out on the street and there was nobody there yet to meet us. Across the street there were a lot of Cubans and in between me and them were a couple of police with guns. One of the people yelled at me, "Are our families in there?"

I said, "Si, si."

I was getting ready to tell them that their families were on their way out when the police got mad and ordered the people back across the street, shooting up into the air.

My traveling companions were still inside in customs when they heard the gunshots. Jim Andrews said, "We have to get out to the street. Marj is out there starting another war."

We finally all got in a van with the Cuban Presbyterians and went to Matanzas to the seminary. We were having a good meeting, but I didn't think I was really seeing Cuba. They had told us to stay on the seminary grounds, but I got up early one morning and thought I would walk to town to see what it was like.

I got down there and people were already lined up trying to buy meat. I took a picture of the line, and somebody came running up, yelling at me in Spanish and wanting to know what I was doing. I ran across the street to a park. They came yelling at me again to tell me to get off the grass. I ran across the street to a butcher shop, not knowing what I was going to do. Along came one of our Hispanic preachers from Texas. He told the people I was just a silly old lady that worked for the church, and they left me alone. I sure was glad to see him that day.

We went to a block meeting while we were there. They called it a block meeting, but it actually encompassed several blocks. I'll never forget that experience either. They had several people get up and tell about what they did about this and what they did about that. I was all right until somebody got up and said, "I'm in charge of how we think." That really bothered me and I just got up and left. I went across the street and saw an elderly woman who lived in a little hubble there. With my little bit of Spanish and her little bit of English, we had a wonderful conversation about Cuba.

That's a very, very troubled land and I don't know what the answers are, but I am very proud that the Presbyterian Church has always been there to help them, and I hope it always will be.

Yes, We Work in Honduras

O h my, did we get shook up in Honduras one time. We met with some groups that were working with Christians who were struggling to help refugees and struggling to keep Christianity alive there.

The Protestant Christians especially were not happy with all the things that were happening there, so we met all day with them. We went to see this wonderful camp that the Protestants were building. I know many of our work groups from the United States have helped build that camp.

We were having a wonderful experience until we got ready to leave. We had been to the U.S. Embassy. Dick Siciliano was the presbyter in Houston then. He unknowingly had some pictures in his briefcase of the Honduran Air Force that somebody had given him in Washington, D.C.

We were getting ready to go into Nicaragua, and the officials found the pictures. They thought he was a spy, so they took him away to talk to him. Some of our group had already gone through customs when Emily Wood came through crying. I asked her what the matter was and she said, "The literature they gave us was communist, and it's in Spanish and I can't even read it."

We were having just a terrible day. But finally we boarded the plane and they let Dick go with us.

He was a basket case, and I asked, "What did they make you do?"

He replied, "Well, I had to give them the names of all of our group and the very first name I thought of was you, Marj—the very first one."

He had forgotten one name and, interestingly enough, that one name was the person who later became a missionary in Central America. I was so thankful that he forgot that name that day. It could have been in their computer forever. The Lord does work in strange ways.

Do We Help Armenians?

O ne of the most unusual things that ever happened to me was when I was on a National Press Women trip to Russia. It had been a unique trip because I had gotten to conduct a press conference at TASS, the very first woman of any nationality to ever get to do that. It was extremely interesting.

We had gone to Georgia to Tblisi and sat around the replica of the table that Stalin and Churchill and Roosevelt sat around to settle the things about World War II. On the last day in that area, the group was looking at a church up the hill. I was tired of hills, and I'd stayed down at a little restaurant and was drinking some Turkish coffee. There was a man sitting there, and I noticed he was wearing a cross. I pointed and said, "Christian?"

And he said, "Armenian."

I said, "Presbyterian."

And he said, "New York."

I've never been from New York, but my father was born in New York State, so I thought, Why not? Why confuse the man? And I said, "Yes."

And he jumped up and said, "Jiniashian, Jiniashian," which is our fund that helps Armenians as they start life in New York.

I said, "Yes!"

And he said, "Uncle, my uncle."

I realized we had helped his uncle, and I said, "Yes!"

He went running to get cognac. As the other women reporters were coming back down the hill, he brought cognac for everyone and wanted them all to drink to the Presbyterian Church. Most of them were Catholics and Baptists and they didn't know what to do about that. So I said, "Just drink to the Presbyterian Church and shut up." And they did. We all saluted the Presbyterian Church, the Jiniashian Fund, and Armenian Christians and how they had survived. I felt very, very proud to be Presbyterian.

Against the Law

I t's against the law in Nepal to be anything but Hindu.
And yet, there's a Catholic and a Protestant church
in Katmandu. Now how did that happen?

Nepal was cut off from the world for a long, long
time. They didn't want any other religions in there and
they said so. When we sent in a group of ecumenical
missionaries, including Presbyterians, they told us to go
home, so we were going home.

One of our Presbyterian missionaries was a bird-
watcher—one of those people who sits around with books
and checks for different kinds of birds in the world. He
was out on his last day watching all those beautiful birds in
Nepal, and darned if the emperor wasn't a bird-watcher
also. They were watching the same bird and they began
talking. The emperor said, "Well, I guess you could stay

here and help with roads and water projects and agriculture."

And the missionary said, "Not unless we could have a church."

"Well, I guess you could have a church in Katmandu if you didn't let it get too big."

So now there are two Christian churches in Katmandu, and they're getting a little bigger every year.

I had a very interesting experience when I was in Katmandu. We were trying to find one of those churches on Sunday night. We never did find the Protestant church but we found the Catholic church and decided to go on in.

I was sitting in the back row and one of the Catholic sisters saw the camera under my chair and came back and called me out. I thought she was going to scold me for having a camera in church. I was starting to apologize and tell her I wasn't going to use it, when she said, "I don't know who you are, but I would like to ask if you could take a picture of this young lad since today is his First Communion. He couldn't come this morning with the group, but he's here tonight and he won't have a picture like the others have."

I said, "If you come and get me when it's time, I will try. I don't have a Polaroid, but if you will give me your address, I'll mail the picture to you."

We agreed on that and I went back to worship.

In the meantime, a big group of Polish Catholics came and filled one whole side of the church. The sister came back and called me up to take the picture. I was up there taking the picture of the little boy, his parents, the priest, and the whole thing, and I heard this kind of rumble over on one side of the church. I found out later the Polish Catholics were just aghast at the ugly American down at the front of the church taking a picture in the middle of the First Communion of this poor child.

Finally, somebody realized what was happening, and the sister went around and told them that she had asked me to take the picture, so they calmed down.

I sent those pictures to Nepal to that Catholic sister and enclosed a card telling where I worked. I got the loveliest letter from her. In it she said, "I don't know how you wandered into our Catholic church, but I'll light a candle for you. I'll bless you forever for those wonderful pictures for that child."

The church is alive and well in the world, and we're all Christians together.

We Must Do Both

When I was in Detroit at a meeting at the beautiful old Fort Street Presbyterian Church, an elder got up and asked me a question that's always difficult to answer — "Why should we help overseas when we have so much need here?"

I bet you've heard that one in your own church. This was a wonderful woman who asked that question. She's an African-American elder who is also a juvenile court judge, and she works with some of the most difficult cases in that very, very tough city. I thought about it a minute and my answer was this: "You're talking about the story of the good Samaritan when our Lord told us to help our neighbor where we are, and I believe in that. But the last thing Jesus told us was to go into all the world and take the gospel to all nations, and I believe in that. And my Bible doesn't say you can do one or the other."

So we have the heavy responsibility of needing to do both. I think each session in each church has to make the decision of how much to do for one and how much to do for the other, not whether to do for one or the other. As a matter of fact, I have found that a lot of times people who don't want to do work overseas don't do much at home either. Sometimes asking that question is just a cop-out.

Ten Lousy Goats

One time when I was in Guatemala, I went along with a driver, two missionaries, and a staff person up a very difficult mountain and through a stream where it looked like we were going to wash away. We finally got to an area where there was a Presbyterian church. It was a strip of land in between major plantations, and they let the farm workers live there. They could eat whatever they could grow, only it was so rocky they couldn't grow much.

The session of the church apparently knew we were coming. They were standing outside of that dirt-floor church, which had no electricity and no glass in the windows. The people had on their best clothes. Three of the men had on rubber boots like our irrigation workers wear, and the rest were barefoot. As soon as we got out of the jeep, they began to thank us. And they thanked us and thanked us.

I thought they were thanking us for coming, but then they brought three little sturdy children out and began to thank us for those children. I was trying to figure out what was going on, and it finally dawned on me. They were thanking us for ten goats that we had provided through a One Great Hour of Sharing offering, and the milk from those goats had saved those particular children.

They took us down the road to see their corn crop because we had given them seed corn. I thought it was pitiful corn, but it did have small ears and they were making tortillas from that corn. So actually, we had given them milk and bread. They thanked us, and thanked us, and thanked us until I was embarrassed to be thanked so profusely for those ten lousy goats.

Have You Ever Been to Cairo?

Cairo is a crowded, dirty city, and the Presbyterians have worked there for a long, long time, especially with schools. We also work with the Coptic Church there. I went to their headquarters one day and a woman there pointed to a tomb and said, "There is Mark's tomb."

And very stupidly I asked, "Mark Anthony?"

And she looked at me in disgust and said, "Mark, Matthew, Mark."

I was stunned. I never stopped to wonder where the writers of the Gospels or the disciples are buried.

Mark was dragged in the streets of Alexandria and beheaded, she told me. I didn't know that. There are so many stories about those early Christians that we have forgotten about or that we never knew at all. We've forgotten that Mary and Joseph and baby Jesus fled to Egypt. I think some Presbyterians think that after Jesus came down off the cross and was resurrected, Christianity moved straight to Scotland and then to Philadelphia. We kind of missed a lot of that early Christian history and the stories of those martyrs.

After that, I began to wonder where the early Christian leaders were, and I found out that James is buried in Spain, John in Turkey, and doubting Thomas in India, where he sold himself as a carpenter's helper so he could help take the gospel to all the world. Of course, Peter is buried in Rome. Where are all those people? Have you ever thought about that?

These were the first missionaries for Christ in the world. What are we doing now?

About Traffic

The traffic was so very bad and the taxi drivers were just running through lights like they weren't even there. I asked the taxi driver, "What does that red light mean to you?"

And he answered me, "The red light means that I can go and the green light means that I must go."

That reminded me of the traffic in Bangkok and the traffic in Manila. In Manila, it takes six hours to get across the city and our mission workers sometimes have to sleep in sleeping bags on the floor of the office because there is no way they can get home and get back in time to do their work.

The Philippines is a country that's going rapidly backward. There are so many problems there. There's the area where they've had the volcano eruptions and whole towns have been wiped out. There are areas where the casino workers are trying to take the good land away from the poor people in a greenbelt outside the city. There's an area where they were trying to get the women out of the red light district, using a Presbyterian Women's Offering for staff workers.

We have all kinds of traffic problems: vehicular traffic and traffic in red light districts. We need to deal with both of these problems. There continues to be such need for the Presbyterian presence in the Philippines.

There Are Street Children Everywhere

We know there are street children everywhere. There are street children in our country. But probably São Paulo, Brazil, and Bogotá, Colombia, have the most street children in the world, though you might have to add Calcutta, India.

We have a missionary couple in São Paulo, Brazil, working with this problem — Bev and Knox Swayze. They're young Princeton graduates. Both of their fathers are Presbyterian ministers. They are there working from before dawn until after dark every day with street children. It is a marvelous mission work.

The synod of the Presbyterian Church in Bogotá works hard trying to get street children out of the dens of thievery there. Children are often left in trash barrels in the city streets for people to find. Often they are found by people who turn them into thieves.

When you're in Bogotá, you have to hang on to everything for dear life because little street children will come up and snatch off your glasses, or your bracelet, or your camera, or your passport, or your billfold. They run so fast you can never catch them. It's a terrible way to raise children. Street children are a special problem in many places, but Presbyterians are working to try to make a difference in the lives of these children.

And in Central America

Central America is a mixed bag. Different denominations do well in different locations in Central America. The Moravian Church does the best job with the Miskito Indians in Nicaragua, and the Presbyterian Church helps with that. The Methodists do the best job in Honduras, and the Presbyterians work with them there.

But we do the best job in Guatemala, where we have over 300 churches. I went to a General Assembly there and it was wonderful. They hang fruits and vegetables over the stage to remind themselves of God's bountiful gifts. At our General Assemblies we rarely think about God's bountiful gifts, but we think a lot about God's bountiful issues.

After that Assembly in Guatemala, I got into a jeep with David Young, a missionary couple, and a driver, and we went to a village they wanted me to see. When we drove into that village, everyone ran. They did not run to us like children do in Africa, bringing wildflowers and waving palm branches, reminding you of what Palm Sunday must have been like. These people ran away from us as hard and as fast as they could go.

I said, "What's wrong here?" All the doors and gates were slamming and there was an instant ghost town, with only one dog left walking in the square.

They told me that the farm workers there had gotten into trouble a few weeks before and the military came to arrest them. They didn't think they would come back alive so they fought with their machetes. Their wives came out and threw pepper into the eyes of the soldiers. The military shot them all down in that square, and they buried them in one big ditch. I saw that ditch. This incident was never reported on our television or in our newspapers.

And as we stood there, one elderly woman came up along the fence close enough that she could call out to us but far enough away that she could run. She called out one word, "¿Presbyteriano?"

I said, "Yes, we're Presbyterians."

As she said, "Come," and she took us to the church.

It bothered me because it's bad enough to be running around the world looking North American without looking Presbyterian. So I asked her, "How did you know we were Presbyterian?"

Her answer is important to all of us. Her answer is scary for all of us. She answered me saying, "Because—because the Presbyterians are the only ones who still come up here to help us."

What if we didn't go? What if we quit going?

Do We Still Have Heroes?

re there still missionary heroes and heroines? The church has had so many martyrs through the years who have been killed by walking the plank, being beheaded, or being shot. We have those who have been whipped and those who have been jailed.

Among those jailed was the Reverend C. M. Kao, General Secretary of the Presbyterian Church of Taiwan, who was once jailed for four years, three months, two weeks, and one day because he had refused to give information about a reporter who wrote derogatory things about the government.

While in jail, Kao wrote a poem about being a caterpillar that turned into a butterfly. Even in jail, Kao brought many people to Christ. The Presbyterian Church of Taiwan sat an empty chair in his spot at the General

Assembly. And the church grew. It has been a strong force in Taiwan.

In recent years, the church has had some tough mission workers—folks like John Haspel, who was taken hostage in Sudan and whipped when he tried to escape and is now in a difficult part of Ethiopia; people like Marge Hoffeld, who went right through a fierce riot in downtown Kinshasha in Zaire to get the passports, cashier's checks, and records of the church out of that country intact.

The missionaries are out there with their lives on the line in many countries—some of which we cannot even talk about. God be with them. We need to remember them in our prayers.

Once the church is in a place, it is never gone. The church is still the light of the world, and we need to remember that *we* are the church.

The Writer

Marj Carpenter retired at the end of 1994 as mission interpreter for the Worldwide Ministries Division of the Presbyterian Church (U.S.A.). Prior to that, she served for fifteen years as manager of the Presbyterian News Service.

Carpenter, a native Texan, has won countless journalism awards in a reporting career that has spanned more than fifty years. Her first job as a cub reporter was for *The Enterprise* in Mercedes, Texas. During her career in the church, she has traveled to nearly 100 countries where Presbyterians have mission work.

Carpenter lives in Big Spring, Texas, where she is a member of First Presbyterian Church.